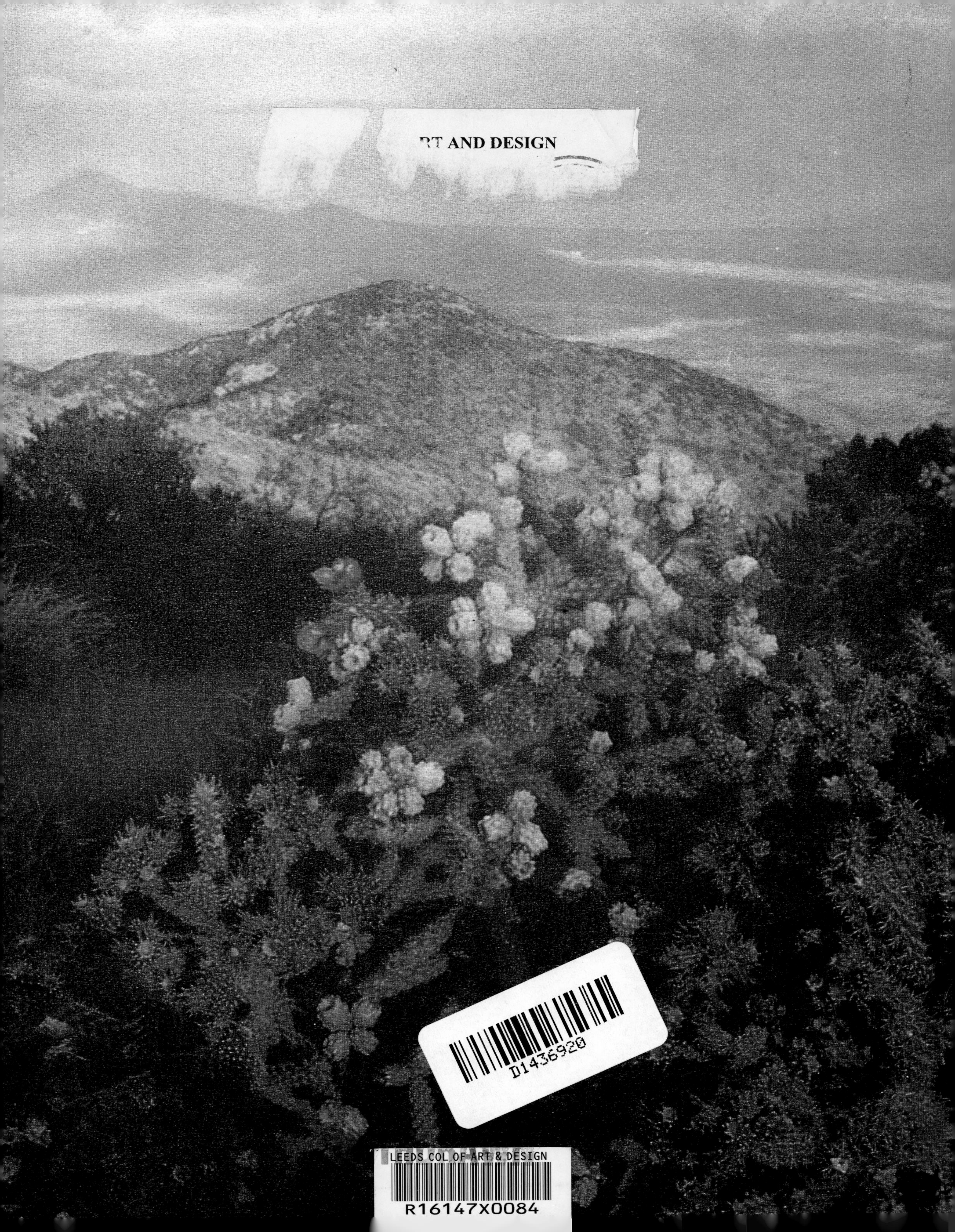

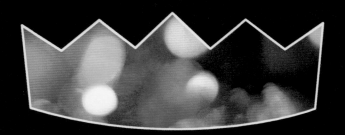

without boundaries

TODD OLDHAM

universe

Frontmatter captions: Front endpapers: *Arizona Highway* magazine, detail complete with staples, 1950s—perfect iconic outdoor moment. Title spread: Opening moment of fashion show, fall 1995. Pages 2–3: Untitled, oil repainting, 1992—I added the animals to this found painting. Page 5: Beaded harlequin pattern, detail, spring 1992. Page 7: Kate Moss, film still, fall 1995. Page 8: APLA poster. Page 9: Detail from found scrapbook, early 1950s. Page 12: Garage Sale Jacket, toaster detail of embroidered pocket, spring 1992. Page 13: Filippa wearing sequined mesh blouse with yarn-fur trim, spring 1995. Interlude captions: Page 65: Hostess Gown, sequined net with fluffy rayon trim, and pants with buttons and Swarovski crystal, spring 1996. Photograph by Ron Contarsy. Page 66: Garage Sale Jacket, hand-embroidered with thread, detail, spring 1992. Page 67: Nicole Kidman wearing prong-set Swarovski crystal wrap skirt and stretch-silk shrunken top, spring 1995. Photograph by Steven Meisel. Page 68: Helena Christensen wearing Broach Dress, glittering with 400 pieces of handmade jewelry created with over 20,000 crystals, fall 1996. Page 69: Garage Sale Jacket, hand-embroidered with thread, spring 1992. Page 70: Muse/icon Billy Beyond wearing Collage Sublimation Print ensemble, spring 1992. Photograph by Michael James O'Brien. Page 71: Lei Bra, embroidered and sequined flowers, detail, spring 1991. Page 72: Bird Top, opalescent sequins and beads on linen, detail, spring 1992. Page 73: Kate Moss wearing Flame Gown, with fabric designed by Tom Bonauro, spring 1994. Photograph by Enrique Badulescu. Page 74: Nadja Auermann and Linda Evangelista wearing matte jersey Bra Gowns, spring 1995. Page 75: Bra Top, detail of embroidery based on jewelry, spring 1992. Page 76: Kate Moss wearing snake-print stretch-charmeuse top, spring 1994. Page 77: Untitled, oil on silver leaf and thread, detail, 1990. Pages 78–79: Naomi Campbell and Anna K. wearing lush texture and pattern mixes with "nuclear rabbit" fake-fur ascots, fall 1996. Page 80: Carolyn Murphy wearing gold nailheads on sheer, flesh-colored gown, fall 1996. Page 81: Bird Top, opalescent sequins and beads on linen for a wrinkled effect, spring 1992. Back endpapers: Color-xerox collage, 1995.

First published in the United States of America in 1997 by UNIVERSE PUBLISHING, a division of Rizzoli International Publications, Inc., 300 Park Avenue South, New York, NY 10010. Copyright © 1997 by Todd Oldham.

97 98 99 / 10 9 8 7 6 5 4 3 2 1

Printed in England. Library of Congress Catalog Card Number: 96-061293. Art direction and design by Tom Bonauro, with assistance from Richard Turtletaub. Unless otherwise indicated, all photographs were taken by Christine Alicino.

Despite all my singular burbling, my success in this funny industry is due to the efforts of many. Words will not properly relay my thanks; but this is a book, so I have to hope they will do.

I wish to thank my friend and mom, Linda Oldham, for her tireless, endless support in all my efforts.

Special thanks indeed to my pal Tony Longoria for intense kindness and inspiration.

Much love and thanks to Jack, Granny, Robin, Brad, and Mikell Oldham for their devotion and patience.

To my dear friend Tom Bonauro, thanks for all the beauty and joy.

Mucho thanks to Jen Bilik for listening to me longer than anyone should have to.

Admiration and thanks to Kevyn Aucoin, Kim Hastreiter, Marylou Luther, John Waters, and Veronica Webb for their kind words and ways.

BIG thanks to Charles Miers, Alex Mairs, Angel Dormer, Cliff Pershes, Conn Brattain, John Roberts, Amanda Goldberg, Billy B., Khoa, Nghia, and Susan S.

Last and absolutely not least, a special thanks to all the photographers, models, stylists, and hair and make-up geniuses with whom I have been blessed to work for their kind and generous assistance with this project.

Any fashion designer who hangs oil paintings by stripper-actress-gun-moll Liz Renay on the wall of his flagship New York store is *my* kind of designer. Todd Oldham knows there is really no such thing as "ugly." Inspired by extremes of every strain of outsider culture, he asks his customers to join him in gleefully breaking fashion rules. Mixing plaids, clashing shades of color, Todd knows

By John Waters

that the sexiest look of all is confidence in your own originality. Instead of the clichéd image of a pretentious, elitist fashion designer, he is the cheerfully driven best friend who makes it easier for people with a sense of humor to get dressed every day. Todd is lucky enough to be able to laugh *with* fashion without making fun of it. Look at the models on his runways—they actually look happy for a change. Susan Sarandon always seems to be beaming whenever

the paparazzi photograph her wearing one of Todd's creations. Even Elizabeth Berkley, fresh from the disaster of "Showgirls," showed her great sense of style by wisely accepting Todd's sincere invitation to model, rehabilitating herself in the media in one quick fashion-show moment. Go to one of Todd's stores and you'll feel like you're hanging out in his living room. Between the great clothes and the witty art, you can't tell where the stock begins and his personal collection ends. Above all, the customers always seem comfortable. You get the feeling even shoplifters would save up their money to buy a Todd Oldham outfit if they could. You can tell by the designs that Todd has always loved a "bad girl." He knows how they can be scary and vulnerable, angry and joyous, and he respects their use of clothes as a weapon against the

Page 13: Filippa wearing sequined mesh blouse with yarn-fur trim, spring 1995. Photograph by Steen Sundland. Above: Untitled, oil re-painting, detail, 1992. Opposite: Mirror Gown, gold bullion and sequins, fall 1991.

14

tyranny of "good taste." By using bad girls' supposed "trashiness" in a liberating way he elevates their fashion defiance to a new kind of elegance: flippant but sensual, garish but graceful—all classes faded into one. Of course, Todd and I don't see eye to eye on everything. I'm extremely right wing on the subject on wearing white before Memorial Day and feel the death penalty is the appropriate punishment. I'm sure Todd delights in the yearly breaking of this old-fashioned commandment and it wouldn't surprise me if he designed an all-white cotton winter line just to prove it. For some reason, he loved the movie *The Sound of Music* as a child, and even though I disagree, I secretly respect his cinematically incorrect militancy on this one. And although I'm convinced someone will make a fortune removing this generation's tattoos, Todd Oldham may be the only man I can imagine at fifty years old wearing his tattoos and *not* looking worn out. Everybody already knows that Todd is a great artist, but I secretly wish he'd become a full-time film director. Just think of what a good "auteur" he could be. He already knows how to run an empire and has reached a broad audience without condescension. He inspires loyalty from his employees, has a vision, and has resisted selling out to the money men. His print ads are better than most movie-stills, his fabrics more clever than many Hollywood costumes, and his fashion shows are as glamorous as the best parties at the Cannes Film Festival. Like all good fanatics, Todd Oldham knows that if you're happily obsessed you'll look great no matter what you wear. He makes success look completely effortless.

Above: Untitled, oil on silver leaf and thread, detail, 1991. Opposite: Detail from found scrapbook, early 1950s. Juxtapositions extraordinaire!

Ann Blyth

Harvey brings Jimmy Stewart an Easter basket. You won't see him in picture, but this is how he probably looks to gentle Elwood Dowd, played by Jimmy in U-I's "Harvey." Jimmy successfully did role on Broadway for some months.

in
spirations

THE CONVERSATIONS IN THIS BOOK TOOK PLACE IN NEW YORK CITY OVER THE SPRING, SUMMER, AND FALL OF 1996.

JEN BILIK: What does creativity mean to you? TODD OLDHAM: I personally find the very notion of creativity to be so liberating and essential. It's a life drive for me. The only reason I do any of this stuff is just because of an internal need to create, no matter what it is. Even if it's just plopping food on your plate, to me it still has to be done in some interesting way. My favorite approach to creativity is to be able create something that only can exist in this moment and referencing a hope for the future by referencing what's been done in the past, what you've done in the past, and bringing the sum of this in the present for the future. Everybody has some plans for it, but nothing is real at that point. It's about making your mark, be it a private mark or a public mark, at this moment, because we're only alive right now. And to be able to pull all that in and make your creative flower bloom is, I think, so exciting. JB: How does that relate to the process? Because a "mark" seems like more of an end. TO: The process is totally unconscious to me. The minute you start questioning or putting in stops or even analyzing exactly why your creativity works, I think you're in the way of it. Why bother thinking when you can do? I believe that creativity comes from a huge, unexplainable pool, so to speak. Creativity is there for everyone; it's just a matter of how much you choose to get in your way or not that determines how much you can tap into this creative source. I choose to not get in my way at all, so for me it comes constantly. JB: Pablo Picasso said, "Once I drew like Raphael, but it has taken a whole lifetime to learn to draw like children." Have you always operated on the principle of getting out of your own way, or have you had to learn to step aside? TO: I've always operated on it because I've always felt it operating. I don't remember making a specific decision. Some people probably have to do it consciously, but for me it's just an M.O. Only as an adult have I been able to articulate how to make it work, to maximize it. I believe that we have every bit of information in the world already in our heads, be it psychic or even tangible things like history. The unknown is more the unaccessed. And then when you discover something, it's like a few blanks have been filled in. I see answers—the most prolific things—come out of children's mouths. Summaries of the universe, off-handed assertions where it's just so clear they know everything that matters. The best thing you can be is like a kid. And I don't mean juvenile, I mean like a kid. All information is in us, it's just what we're taught to forget and what we learn to forget. That's where the obstacles come up. And

especially I think it's probably harder to be a creative person now than it was two hundred years ago, even thirty years ago, because the outside influence is so strong that you really have to be either very grounded or, in my case, almost like an idiot savant to be able to participate in any creative arenas. JB: When you pull different tangible elements together, like when you create your prints and you incorporate, say, a wood grain that comes from a tree, or a Moroccan tile pattern, or a roadscape, isn't that pulling from the tangible rather than a group consciousness? TO: Tangible elements help to personalize our creativity. You can usually pick out a Picasso among a group of paintings, in part because what you're seeing are pieces of Picasso's vernacular. Or in my case, you're seeing a piece of

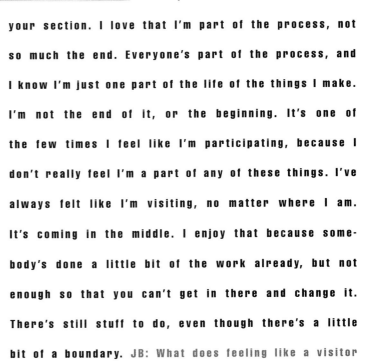

my vernacular, which is comprised of things from my history on the planet at this moment. I saw, for example, open Texas roads as a kid. I know what that stuff looks like, and certain things moved me as a child— I probably didn't even know it at the time, but I just felt happy inside. So we create these almost superhero versions of what sticks with us. I love the freedom of being and coming from outside, I love the inspiration of being an outsider, I love the reverence for it, but how do I help to create something tangible that maybe can excite someone else? And I have a boundary, a very loose boundary called "clothes"—how do I approach it? I call

on my life's storage bank to help me personalize my version of creativity. I start with something that moves me. My life experience is the filter that all the creativity comes through. So I'm happy that my life-experience filter is really big, and I've had exposure to a lot of different stuff. That's what's so wonderful about creativity—even though it's all coming from this one source, by no means are we going to get the same result from everybody. We're getting our own special personalized versions of it, which is so great. JB: I like the idea that despite individual differences, creativity comes from one common source, because it takes the pressure off in terms of feeling like it's all about you and your ability to invent original expression from scratch. If it's all flowing, you can kind of step into it. TO: You're just in your section. I love that I'm part of the process, not so much the end. Everyone's part of the process, and I know I'm just one part of the life of the things I make. I'm not the end of it, or the beginning. It's one of the few times I feel like I'm participating, because I don't really feel I'm a part of any of these things. I've always felt like I'm visiting, no matter where I am. It's coming in the middle. I enjoy that because somebody's done a little bit of the work already, but not enough so that you can't get in there and change it. There's still stuff to do, even though there's a little bit of a boundary. JB: What does feeling like a visitor

Pages 22–23: Photograph from the *Fort Worth Star Telegram*'s archive, 1960s—truly subversive-mundane photography at its worst-best. Above: Top of Paper-Doll Box Number 2, early 1940s. Opposite: Dreampet, 1950s—about 200 Dreampet models were made; they remind me of Andy Warhol, and I find them stylistically charming and weird, sort of cuddly-scary.

MAHA RATH
AGARBATHI

जय रथ
अगरबत्ती

INDIAN INCENSE STICKS

King of
Jasm

HIGHLY PERFUMED
MADE IN INDIA

SAMADHI
AGARBATTI

ROSE
BATHI

कल्याण
रोज़

mean to you? TO: When I was a kid in the States, before we moved to Iran, I never fit in very well at all. I didn't have much in common with anybody else and felt baffled all the time. Those activities, those thought muscles, they just didn't go with me—my gear didn't fit into the rest of the gears. It wasn't until we moved overseas that I started to like myself. Everything was strange, so I felt more a part of it. It felt right to be in those other circumstances. Ever since then I've led my life in that manner, to be a visitor no matter where I am, to celebrate the joy of duality, to celebrate the joy of differences. Ever since then it's been okay. JB: Did it bother you not to fit in? "Baffle" is a pretty benevolent word, and the social torture of not fitting in could probably be attributed to much of the childhood psychological pain we carry with us. TO: I felt more like an observer than a victim of circumstances. But I had my family, and they were my friends; I didn't really need a lot of other friends. It's good that the way I think about myself happened organically, but I realize that it's a necessity for me because the only way to function well is to be a happy visitor. It's a healthy way to go about it. It's tough to survive, you know? A lot of people don't make it very well. We've created a very complicated structure for our world. People who share my points of view rarely integrate themselves into commerce or mainstream systems and they just remain as outsiders. So I have a really odd view of things because I partici-

pate in these mainstream systems, and yet hang on to every shred of my own version of it. That's why I think the creative process can be such a great educational tool. Applying creativity to an already set-up form really teaches you to stretch your mind. Because so many of the things I deal with are pretty much subjective, and anything could go a million different ways, charting your way through really is a matter of looking at things immediately with a 360-degree view, compiling what's going to be the way to do it, and then knowing how to go. It's problem-solving 101— how you see when you're corralling. Imagine how a kid's mind could work when he or she is having to relate to a difficult personal situation, yet with the knowledge of how to take something from beginning to end, and the ability to make sure that it's fueled by this thing we don't really know about. It's liberating to be able to live through that. JB: It's almost like what a lot of people call confidence. TO: Maybe that's what it is, because I've never not had confidence. It never occurred to me that you should really listen to what anybody else says. Yeah, once you strip that back it really is confidence. Especially when I see people who've had rough childhoods, or their dads told them they couldn't draw, they had to play sports and stuff . . . I never had any of that. I totally lucked out to have all creativity supported. JB: What's the difference between ego and confidence? TO: I think that ego is a by-product of a lack of confidence. They almost

Opposite: Incense packages, 1980s—gorgeous imagery with flawlessly flawed printing. Above: Contemporary Indian miniature, made from Ganges River clay—I have a great "soulular" love of Indian imagery.

seem more like polar opposites. I think you're born with confidence, but ego is acquired. Usually the least talented people have the biggest egos—I see that when I step out of my own little working environment to consult for huge megacorporations. I've met a lot of difficult personalities and I've encountered many rules that are unnecessary and confusing. I just find a whole general sadness by all that. Commerce is a weird thing. It can complicate things if you don't understand what it is. I see so many systems that are solely based on hierarchy and judgment of others, on emphasizing differences between workers and bosses. The more you can create your own systems outside of existing systems, the more creativity will bloom. Systems are changing, though. There are enough people like me and you around now who are so disinterested in the way

things are supposed to be done that we're not even interested in changing them. We're changing things simply by not being a part of them. You don't have to fight against it—you can just simply not be it, and those other systems will cannibalize themselves. I think it takes a lot of ego removal to be conscious of your participation in the larger whole, and I'm really happy that I've never really had ego problems. I don't mind what anybody says about the stuff I do or think. It doesn't make that much difference to me. JB: For so many people, it seems difficult to move away from caring about what others think, to move away from being so self-conscious. TO: It's just opinions, you know. I'm really clear on that. That's why criticism means nothing to me, because you have to see something for yourself. Although I tell you, really bad reviews will make me go see something, because I know that if a chord has been struck so strongly, then there's something there. Good reviews to me are scarier, or seem less real than horrible reviews, which intrigue me. It's passion! And there's so much basic mediocrity in mainstream successes. But of course things get homogenized when you have to please everyone. Then again, I've definitely seen some sad examples of what critics can do to people when they really buy into it, when it really matters to them. Their spirits get broken eventually, and their creativity can be so crippled. But on the other hand—a while ago some foreign magazine came in, and there was an article on this potter, Beatrice Wood, who was 103 years old. I couln't read the article because it was in another language, but I could see so much inspiration on this woman's face, it was amazing—103 years old, and radiant. Totally radiant and delightful and pleased. I tore it out and put it right on my bulletin board, because I thought, this is an inspiration. I don't really know her

Above: Untitled, Ellen Berkenblit, gouache on board, 1984—one of my painting heroes, whom I actually know. Opposite: Hand-beaded flowers, 1992—gift made by my mom, Linda Oldham.

work, I don't know her politics, I don't know her life so much, but you can just see on her face that she's had a fulfilled life. What more could you hope for? And to see her beautifully stained and wrinkled hands manipulating the clay. She's found joy in what she does, and that's probably why she's 103 and still smiling. I see so many people get to that age and they have no interest in living at all—not even that age, but thirty years younger, or even thirty years old. They're dormant. JB: I think the dormancy comes from boredom. TO: Oh, that's the worst. Boredom is certainly the opposite of life drive. Once that's set in, where else do you go after boredom? But how could you be bored? Though I suppose it takes a brave person to never cave to boredom. I'm sure I would get a lot of shit for the way I am if I weren't blessed and lucky enough to be in the situation that I'm in, and to

have such a support system around me. I'm really lucky because I have a lot of jobs, and a lot of outlets for my creativity, and I know it's all because I don't think about it—I just do. I know the feeling physically in my body that comes from thinking too much, and it's the same one I had with homework as a kid. It's because there was too much obligation to learn and stress out over all that stuff. Now, whenever I have that feeling, the homework feeling, I know I'm absolutely really screwing it up, I'm in the way of this good experience. So step aside and enjoy yourself. JB: Even if you're doing what you

want to do, there's still a huge gap between having an idea and doing something about it. There's the reality of showing up every day. TO: That doesn't feel like work to me. It's not about working hard, it's about working often. I don't mind being busy. The only efforts that bother me are those where the process doesn't amount to something. But the best part of my work is that I still feel unemployed, my favorite feeling in the world. JB: Is that because it's by choice, doing what you love to do? TO: Oh yeah. I love to be able to express myself. I wouldn't necessarily work if I didn't have to. Who would, though? But I would still be very, very busy. JB: In terms of moving toward what you like to do, isn't the challenge sometimes that it can be difficult to know yourself, know what you want, and therefore know what kind of choices to make? TO: Even if you don't know all those things, you know enough that you can at least take a baby step. And often it just takes getting your toe in the pond before you know what the reality of the entire pond is. I certainly don't know everything that I want. I do vacillate on some things, but it's always better just to do something. And if your mind is set up to sort of minimize potential disasters, then it kind of works. My life is not here because I had a lot of money and I got to do what I wanted; I come from a broke family. It's all just because it somehow worked out and I never really compromised on what to do.

Above and opposite: Details from beautifully distressed found scrapbooks, early 1950s.

Ava Gardner ————— Jam

Having worked with Todd for many years, I have come to realize that our kinship originates beyond our related lines of work. From early ages, we both used our creativity as salvation from a mainstream world in which we didn't completely fit. Through our artistic endeavors, we were able to find great comfort and joy, and with encouragement from our families, our creativity flourished. One of my earliest memories is of myself as a young toddler sitting with my mother and a couple dozen wooden blocks in the living room of our Lafayette, Louisiana, home. She was trying to teach me about color by cheerfully saying "blue!" and asking me to find the correct block, but the only one that held any interest for me was long, cylindrical, and fuchsia. No matter what color my mother asked for, I inevitably handed her that bright magical column. I carried that fuchsia wooden block around with me for a very long time; it brought me great comfort and the men in my family great concern. It seemed my predetermined role models were to be John Wayne, George Wallace, and my father's father, whose affinity for tickling me until I couldn't breathe, among other charming qualities, made me somewhat apprehensive about becoming an adult male. By the time I was six or seven years old, my younger brother, Keith, was being touted as the perfect example of a healthy young boy. His idea of a fun day was shooting at any moving creature in our backyard (including me), tearing things apart to see how they worked (like my new tape recorder, which I bought with my birthday money), and destroying my hand-built, deluxe, two-story Lego home, complete with pool and terrace. The gap between his and my versions of "male" seemed one even Evel Knievel could not bridge—a point that was constantly driven home to me by my family, school, church, and television. Sunday nights were often the worst. Not only had I been forced to practice baseball (I would rather have rubbed broken glass into my eyes) the day before, but I had endured the rantings and ravings of our homophobic closet-case priest that morning. Later on that evening you could always find me arguing with my father and brother over whether we were going to watch *M*A*S*H* or *Sonny and Cher*. Guess which one I wanted to watch. It was around this time that I discovered that arts and crafts were my passion. With my mother's support, I went from macramé to wood burning to sand art to candle making to glass cutting to string art to copperwire jewelry to doll making to painting—leaving in my wake some of the most ghastly creations human eyes had ever laid rest upon. My par-

ents were on a tight budget, but my mother always seemed to find a way to help fund my "art." Although a few years earlier she had been reprimanded for allowing me to buy a pair of lime green patent-leather penny loafers (as my father put it, "those goddamned girls' shoes," which they were), my mother consistently supported my artistic endeavors. She quietly understood that I was indeed "different" but not necessarily "bad," and that my creativity was the only outlet I had to transform my frustrations about not fitting in into something useful, something that helped me feel that I had value. In 1978, at the age of sixteen, I convinced my mother to make clothes for a "play" my friends were putting on—as if quitting school and moving in with my eighteen-year-old boyfriend, Glenn, weren't enough, I now had my mother making gowns for the local drag queens. ("Aren't there any girls in any of these plays?" she asked.) As the early 1980s rolled around and punk and new wave were all the rage elsewhere, Lafayette remained a replica of 1950s Mayberry. After my friends Scottie (a beautiful transsexual) and Dana (a lesbian with a crew cut and army fatigues) and I (black lipstick and a long white streak in my hair) were not allowed into the local gay bar ("Y'all are dressed too weird—y'all are gonna ruin it for the rest of us"), I started to realize that even our own were against us. And since the demand in Louisiana department stores for male makeup artists was right up there with black Jewish paraplegic lesbian mountain climbers, I decided to move. As usual, my mother helped out, convincing my father to buy my boyfriend's car (which they didn't need and couldn't afford) so we could have $1,500 to move to New York City. When the money ran out (two weeks later) my mother scraped her pennies together to help us make ends meet, always believing that I would someday succeed. Her tireless faith got me through some of the most difficult times in my life. When I finally got my first big break (Steven Meisel booked me to do makeup for a *Vogue* shoot), I called my mother and together we cried with joy. From her patience with those wooden blocks to her "oohs" and "aahs" over the pastel drawings of Barbra Streisand I did as a teenager, all the way to her work for more than a decade with Parents and Friends of Lesbians and Gays, my mother has taught me what creativity, inspiration, and love are all about. Her respect for and celebration of my uniqueness gave me the ability to believe in myself, to take chances, and, ultimately, to be willing to fail in order to succeed. —Kevyn Aucoin

Page 32: *Mike*, oil on gold leaf, detail, 1990. Page 33: Shoshana, fall 1993. Above: Zipper pull, 24-karat gold plate with Swarovski crystal, fall 1992. Opposite: Tyra Banks wearing embroidered Mirror Gown with patterns inspired by Indian textiles, fall 1993.

JB: When you're walking down a busy street, what do you tend to focus on? TO: I notice details. I probably wouldn't notice the five-hundred-pound woman coming at me, but I would notice the texture that the sidewalk, her shoe, and her pant created, or that her hands were moving like I once saw a tank of squids moving in Japan. My visual memory's impeccable. What I hear and remember is very weak. It's the delight of having my eyes tickled, which is something I strive for in my work, that I might amuse your eyes, or excite your eyes. If you look without judgment, and see with inspiration, for me that's just kind of it. And because that happens, I don't get caught up in . . . maybe what I'm seeing on the sidewalk is a piece of paper stuck in dog shit next to warmed-over antifreeze, yeah—but look at the way it stuck! Have you ever seen a more phosphorescent green in daylight? There are things to celebrate about everything. It's just how you choose to go about it. JB: That antifreeze in the gutter is beautiful, but scary at the same time because the color is so inorganic. Maybe not in algae, but in a New York City gutter? It's a seductive, dangerous beauty. Do you see the danger? Does it make the beauty any less? TO: It has to coexist. How would we know beauty without what we term as ugly? But is ugly not beautiful? There are endless questions about these things. I just try to see . . . ugly to me is unattractive behavior. But I've never really seen an ugly person. JB: Did visual things stick with you when you were a kid? TO: It's definitely visual details that create my timeline memory. I believe that we retain the new information we need. If something interests me, it sticks forever, but if it doesn't . . . and it's always been that way. The first thing I can remember really noticing in terms of movement and color was this toy that consisted of all these wonderfully translucent colored disks with slits that you slid into each other to build whatever you wanted. There was a pink disk and an orange disk, and it was like, pink and orange, pink and orange—something was different with pink and orange. I'd just sit there for hours, putting pink on orange, putting pink under orange, looking through pink and orange. They were beautiful. Then I got the flashlight and held it through the pink and orange and looked at the reflection. It was like being given a special gift that day to be able to see the way color can thrill. And it's something I've carried with me. I can't tell you how many collections I've done with pink and orange next to each other. It still tickles my eyes, but maybe I'm overassuming that others might be tickled by it too. They probably are, in its wrongness. You can create wonderful, lively friction with color, you know, just the combinations. Lime green and purple are so exciting together, don't you think? It's like a guaranteed party. JB: From moving around a lot, physical places must have had a big visual effect on you. TO: I was born in Texas, but I don't remember a lot until California, just bits and pieces. JB: What about living in Iran? TO: The first time I ever noticed this specific kind of color was in Iran, at the bazaar. We would go shopping there, and if you wanted spices you'd scoop them with a shovel out of these enormous burlap bags with contents so dense—imagine every incredible gorgeous spice. They were like big polka dots of color, but the kind of color was for me the most thrilling of all: curries, paprika, cumin, saffron. To see those shades that obviously relate to each other, but one brings in a fluorescent quality, one brings in a sort of a muddy quality—I see that as something I relate to all the time when I create tonal effects and feel the thrill of putting off-shades together. JB: Have you ever noticed clashes, or only what pleases your eye? TO: The clash pleases my eye. JB: Do you ever see anything where you don't like the way it goes together? TO: It's more that a lot of times my most frustrating thing to see is when colors aren't as lovely as they could be. Obviously reaction to color is all subjective. For me to say it's rotten means nothing other than it's rotten to me. I remember when I was a kid having on a pair of khaki pants and a gray sweatshirt, and just marveling at how great those two colors looked together. But why *would* they look good? They don't share anything, there's no pattern—it didn't go, but yet it totally went.

So that was one of the first times I thought about how the sum of color vibration is more interesting than the vibrations on their own, as individuals. JB: I've always been amazed that no matter what colors they are, flowers always go together. Whereas there are lots of times when it feels like synthetic colors don't harmonize. What's the difference? TO: The lack of judgment. We're charmed by flowers' inherent beauty, and often by their fragrance—which can be highly hypnotic. So we cut them a lot of slack. We don't have those preconceived notions. Synthetic colors are generally applied to specific arenas—decorating, furniture, clothing—so we go in with strong judgments about what's accessible, what works. Because I look at everything more as flowers, that's maybe why I'm able to combine things, and it's that conviction that somehow wins people over. JB: But you also never lose potential with natural colors—and they're so much more complex. TO: Oh, truly. Because they're not single colors, they're amalgams. It's a mishmash of color. Plus, in natural situations, the play of light has so much to do with how we see. And natural color has depth and texture—far more physical depth and texture than synthetic color. So we're thrilled by the way the light's behaving and it's just so much more lively and fun. But with synthetic colors, it's the flatness that's the charm. I like that it's been filtered. You have to celebrate that it's a different version of it.

Left: Chrystelle wearing sporty ensemble, spring 1994. Right: Naomi Campbell wearing hand-beaded Mandarin Vest, spring 1994.

There's no way I could match a pink to that gorgeous flower on the vine out there. There's just no way, so don't try to compete. All synthetic colors are just homages to natural colors, anyway. It's like when I have beading done in India. I send over my pattern, but I know that through the artisans' hands, I'm going to get something else back that isn't exactly what I thought of at first, but it's almost always great. JB: How wonderful to trust that freedom. It means you always have surprises. TO: Yeah, you look forward to the surprise. Surprises are almost always great. And you especially get surprises when you break rules. There are lots of preconceived notions about color, but every one of them's wrong. When I was about nine, my grandmother told me to go back in the house and change out of my blue jeans and green tank top, because they didn't go together. I remember feeling utterly astonished, because it was so laughable to me that you would have to go change your clothes, which I never want to do anyway, and put on something else because somebody said it didn't go together. What are you talking about? I have it on! JB: There are a bunch of color rules, like redheads aren't supposed to wear pink. TO: Which they look divine in. I don't know if it was that I always kind of appreciated bad girls and troublemakers and that sort of thing, but any time there was a rule or a law, I would spend much time thinking about why—why would somebody think like that, and

what would be the alternative to it? What rules? There are all sorts of dumb rules, all of them wrong. Even the stuff like horizontal stripes make you look fat. Totally wrong. Clothes that make you look fat make you look fat—it's not the horizontal stripes. And I don't see why there's anything wrong with looking fat. JB: I'm always really pleased when I see toddlers who have so obviously dressed themselves, wearing polka dots and plaids and stripes, all at once, and certainly nobody ever intended them to go together. They've got no common colors whatsoever—no Garanimals trick behind that outfit. But there's such glee to it! TO: Isn't the ultimate goal achieved if the person who has it on is having a nice time? That's all that matters when you're talking about something as silly as clothes. It's how you feel. Dressing or designing is really about understanding your goal in the outcome of an outfit. Is it to make the person feel sexy or to help amplify a sexy thought they're having? Is it to make them cozy, comfortable, invisible, apparent? What is it? JB: What do you think is stylish? TO: To me, real style is always in the more eccentric personalities, those who are doing what they're really excited about rather than following what's in style. When I think of "styled" as a description, I picture a person looking like something a magazine recommends for this month. It's more a mimicking of popular trends than it is an expression of individuality. When you see people who

Opposite: Collage of fashion-show invitations. Above: My private stationery with Tuft Print, detail.

are so singular in their style, there's nothing more thrilling, because you know there's so much behind it. JB: And what do you find sexy? TO: What turns me on isn't the traditional stuff. I think a person is far more than what we consider to be the sexy bits. It's much more about the way somebody moves, the fluidity of actions. Provocative dressing is not necessarily sexy. I'm drawn to contradiction, to nontraditional versions of sexiness: I have a female friend who wears men's underwear. Or another friend who will show up in a housedress, with nothing on underneath, and a pair of flip-flops. Or once I saw this girl in the East Village—she had on a white men's tank top, and her skirt was another tank top, black with the *Batman* logo on it. She had just put it on upside down, with the armholes hanging against her hips, and added a belt. She looked fantastic. That was sexy; that was really sexy. JB: In terms of that contradiction, I once read a very good line about punk rockers, that their look simultaneously says "Look at me" and "Fuck you—what are you looking at?" TO: Oh, that's great. Punk rockers are my favorite members of society. They're like very interesting tribes. When I did a fabric based on fractals about three years ago, somebody took the print and showed it to the man who discovered the fractal, and he thought it was wonderful. His comment was, "What an exciting tribal use of the medium." I loved that—here I thought I was using the most sophisticated imagery, and to him it was a tribal application. JB: It doesn't take much confidence to wear simple, noncontradictory things, but you have to be pretty gutsy to carry off a contradiction. Is that what appeals to you? TO: That's probably what I find sexy, when you boil it all down. I also enjoy exploring regions of the body that are not necessarily what we consider to be traditionally sexy. At the same time, I have a great fascination with breasts, but not in the normal way. I'm always highlighting them graphically with shapes and prints. I like them as punctuation points in an outfit, and I love direct emblems. But maybe that's just a rebuttal to what you're not supposed to do—don't put things here! JB: While at the same time, everybody's always trying to puff them up and push them out to make them as noticeable as possible. TO: There are so few things that physically define gender, so why not celebrate them? I don't think I've ever done anything exploitative. I'm always baffled at the way that modesty and propriety have tied up so much of the way women view themselves. It's confusing to me. JB: I like your breakdown of sexy, cozy, comfortable, invisible, apparent. They don't have any judgment calls. TO: No, no. You're supplying tools to help people sort of make it through the day in some way. So with that in mind, just consider those aspects that we like to express.

Above: UFO photos, black-and-white Polaroids taken for *SoHo Journal*, 1994. Opposite: Helena Christensen wearing Muffler Dress, fall 1994—Fair Isle made very sexy. Pages 44–45: Psychedelic paisley sequined and bead-embroidered gown, detail and full view, fall 1993. Pages 46–47: Hand-embroidered and beaded skirt with patterns based on ancient Egyptian motifs, full view and detail, spring 1993.

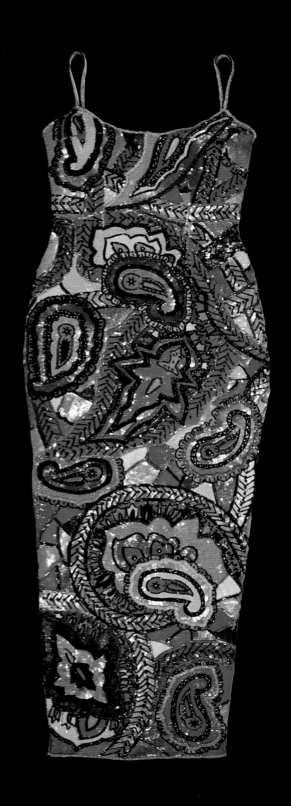

Structure

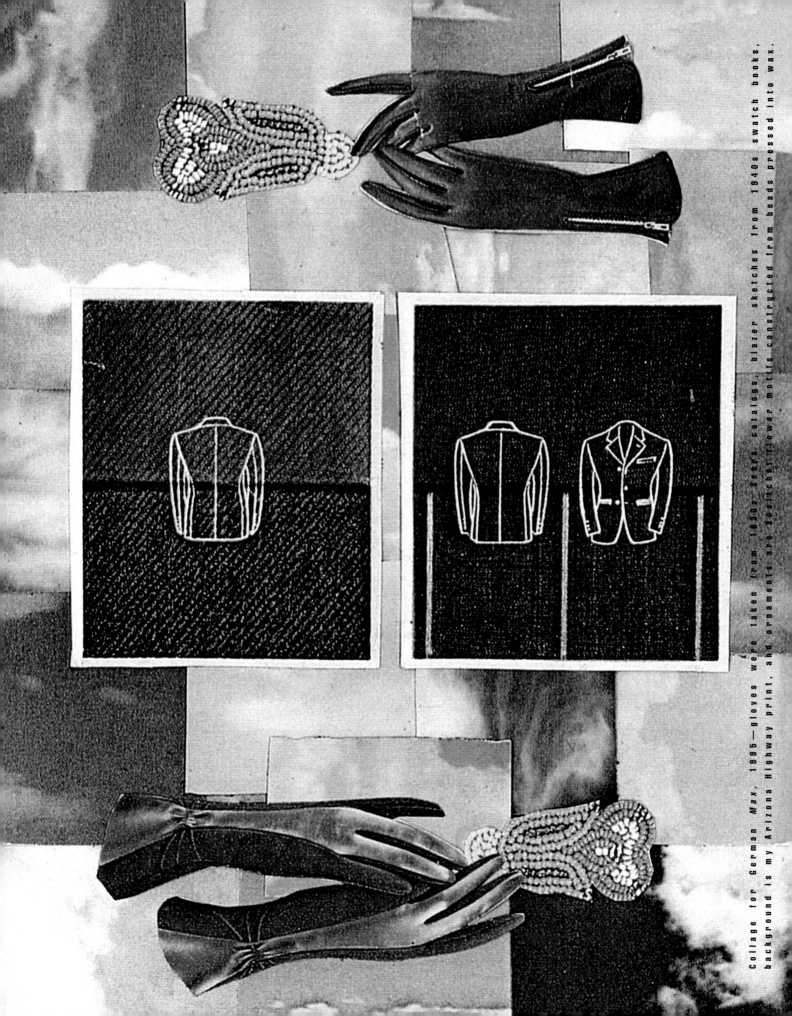

Sourcing Todd Oldham's creativity is like dowsing for water with a divining rod—by the time you locate one source, the rod, or Todd, has revealed another. When I first met Todd in 1990, I thought his anima derived from his uncanny psychic abilities. He *knew* what to design because he *knew* what was coming next. Fashion by precognition. Once he called me from the company factory in Dallas to ask if I was all right. He was worried because he'd dreamt that I caught my false eyelashes in a zipper. (I hadn't, but I did have conjunctivitis.) Todd also knew we had met before—probably during his favorite past life, when he was a 1940s housewife ("There's no other way I would know that era the way I do") and I was a teenage baton-twirler. I thought our first meeting was somewhere on the Mississippi River when he was Huck Finn and I was either Mark Twain or Becky Thatcher. Todd's cosmic connections are also influenced by the fact that he's on the extreme cusp of Libra. This probably explains his long-held extremist contention that he can't imagine wanting to get in the middle of *anything.* As any good astrology buff knows, the symbol of Libra is the scales. A Libran's life is a balancing act in a search for universal justice. To this end, Todd knows how to weigh the evils of the sometimes supercilious world of fashion against the good it can do, as in using his celebrity—or, as he prefers, his public voice—to support AIDS charities and animal rights. Todd's vibes resound in his MTV segments, which stand out in the sometimes exasperating coverage of fashion on television. As Todd puts it, "TV has desensitized people to the pompous aspects of fashion because you can't mask on TV. And as more and more people see the inner workings of fashion with their very own eyes it becomes more democratic." For his first "Todd Time," he took his audience on a three-minute thrift-shop tour, where his chance encounters included what he called a surreal confrontation with "a woman who had so many false eyelashes clumped on and about her eyes I had a hard time making eye contact." (False eyelashes are a continuing thread here.) He recovered quickly enough to show such smart shopping tactics as looking on the floor whenever you see an empty hanger ("You can't put stuff on hold at a thrift shop, so customers find their own way of protecting their treasures until they can come back with more money"); checking out the men's suit racks when you're looking for a woman's jacket; inspecting all good-looking pants regardless of size ("Those size forty-eight pants in mint condition will make a great pair of paper-bag pants when belted around your size thirty-six waist"); and carefully examining two-piece outfits ("The bottom may have a terrible spot, but the top could be perfect—and vice versa"). If you've read this far, you know that Todd Oldham has a sense of humor. This wellspring of creativity is evidenced in his clothes, which he makes out of everything from cork to pot holders, Persian and sisal rugs to drawer-pulls and mirrors inspired by those in his bedroom. He once concocted a miniskirt with a beaded panel of *Mona Lisa* on the front and a Picasso-like flip lady on the back. The flip side was duplicated from a portrait he found in a thrift shop. While many designers are inspired by fabric and begin their design process with the selection of fabrics, Todd takes the act of creativity one step farther. He invents most of his own fabrics, designing his own prints, placing his own inlays, sourcing his own decoupage, and, in the case of his now-famous Mosaic Dress, photoprinting a polyester gabardine fabric with 1,755 computer-generated colors without one single repeat. (The mosaic in the dress was replicated as the backdrop for Todd's spring 1996 runway show.) Todd's passion for crafts, which he's been doing since his granny taught him to sew at age nine, is best seen in his boutiques in New York's SoHo, Miami's South Beach, and on Los Angeles's Beverly Boulevard, where his work is evidenced in floors covered with shellac-coated pages torn from old books, desks created from broken tiles, dressing rooms wallpapered in pages from flower and bird books, and chandeliers made from coiled copper wire wrapped around broken glass and crystals, topped with tiny lampshades. Perhaps the essential source of Todd's creativity is his fearlessness. He's not afraid to explore the world beyond the runway. He's not afraid of the big bad wolves in the fashion press. He's not afraid to work with his family. And he's not afraid to admit that he'd probably like to leave the fashion world one day in favor of filmmaking. As he says, "I'll work with a camera instead of a sewing machine." —Marylou Luther

Above: Beaded button, fall 1990. Opposite: Silk Caged-Waist Dress, spring 1992. Photograph by Michele Clement.

JB: Do you think your work is uniquely American? TO: Absolutely. American stuff provides my most solid reference point, especially what people consider to be great American sportswear. Plain stuff—plain pants, plain jackets. Though I think that Americans perceive Europe to be more sophisticated, a stronger harbinger of taste. I love so much of what's uniquely American—our craft history, Americana. But we chose terrible colors for our flag. JB: What would you have chosen? TO: For a nation, you need green in the flag because you have to project safety and health. White's always nice, and then maybe turquoise, with a little bit of red for passion and creativity. If you're going to create a country, those would be really good color vibrations to rule a country by. JB: If you were designing the flag for the first time, what would it look like? TO: It would definitely be circles. Those stripes we have are too rigid. I think concentric rings would be better, like a bull's-eye, to show clarity and to communicate a never-ending, embracing quality. We would do better with a circular motion instead of those regimented stripes. And I'd make the flag really big. Wouldn't it be fun if it was really, really huge? JB: Like a Christo version of a flag! Would there be anything else besides a really big set of concentric turquoise, green, red, and white circles? TO: We could use some encouraging motif. Personally, I'd like to see

a little dog in the middle, but a tree might be a good national symbol of strength, perseverance, and fortitude. I don't think the flag needs to be so nationalistic, but instead more spiritual in its motifs. Having circles is a good start for that—much better than stars or stripes. We did really blow it on our flag. It doesn't show much hope or optimism because it's so static. Just the shapes it uses—they don't create any sense of prosperity. It's a bad design to represent a country's interests, in my opinion. JB: On a more theoretical note, do you think your eclecticism is uniquely American? TO: Our country is the biggest melting pot in the world, so yeah, my eclecticism comes from the appreciation of the simultaneity of it all. Because we don't have huge, singular religious or cultural histories, we've had options since the beginning, so of course our version of it is going to be a beautiful jumble of simultaneous sensibilities. No place is better at that than America, and no city better than New York. No place is as multi-everything as New York. JB: What to you is the definition of kitsch? TO: To me it's not so much the definition that matters, because the reality of what people think kitsch is and the actual definition don't seem to be fully related. It's a catchall for lowbrow references. And there are so many great things in what we term as lowbrow reference points already, so it's just sad to see them

Pages 52–53: Amber Valetta and Kate Moss wearing double-faced duchesse-satin evening coats sewn inside out, spring 1996.

reduced to an inspirationless, lazy word. Kitsch. I have appreciation for the so-called lowbrow, but I incorporate an entire range of elements, whether high or low, and it comes out my version. JB: So kitsch is uninterpreted and unmingled, just thoughtless reproductions of lowbrow references? TO: It is. One of the reasons I love the more lowbrow stuff is because behind it are some of the happiest, most free people in the world. So many middle-class neighborhoods are nervous about what the neighbors might think if somebody wants to paint their house lime green. But often trailer parks, or really low-income situations, are just full of beautiful, wild anything! JB: I think erroneous kitsch designations stem partly from the presence of whimsy and humor, because you more often find those traits in lowbrow stuff than in fine art. TO: For me, it's important to make things that are fun but not funny. I don't want people to laugh at clothes, or laugh at people wearing different things. To smile, or to be amused by, is nice. Whimsy is good. It shows lightness, it shows spontaneity, all the things I like in my life. Whimsy has to be grounded in a good idea, because often people think of it as temporary or frivolous. I like to consider whimsy more as a sensibility, to be able to place things lightly, to arrive and say "Aha!" and have your arrangement be right. Some people would say that's whimsical, others might say it's trust.

JB: There seems to be a puritanical prejudice against artistic things being pretty or fun, as if they wouldn't be worthy of attention, such that you don't often see intelligence applied to those qualities. It's the effort to get oneself taken seriously, as if getting taken seriously is about being serious. TO: Why is it so important to be taken seriously? JB: When you take all these prints and put them together, they always make some sense, as opposed to someone randomly throwing on a few different plaids and polka dots. What makes that work? TO: There are psychological dynamics involved in design. Even though all the color looks really spontaneous, there's great thought that goes into the combinations. It's knowing how to go with that visual thrill, that tickle that comes from seeing the combinations, knowing not to get into the judgment but to go for the emotion. A while ago people started to ask me how I combined patterns, and I had to give real answers, so it forced me to think about what it is that I do that makes it "work" somehow. And I say "work" in quotations, because there are plenty of people who want to throw up when they see my stuff. The trick is sharing two or three color palettes within the prints, and it's a matter of scale and proportion. It's a matter of making a few elements match, so it doesn't bounce off your eyes; it can go in your eyes and give your brain a second to say, "Oh, all right, I can understand."

Opposite and above: Skirt, intricately embroidered with gold bullion and thread in Persian rug patterns, front and back, fall 1991.

But I really appreciate the psychological complications of it. And it's not just visual tricks—you can put things together by concept. I once did an outfit with prints I reinterpreted from Egyptian tomb paintings. The prints didn't show too many of the same colors, but because they came from the same thought process, they somehow worked. That's rare. JB: Especially because they're non-Western and non-American, the prints seem more alike to us despite the different colors. TO: It's interesting the way that works. I approach it without any thought process at all, but it's a subtle form of manipulation to link it together enough that people can get it. I think of it as instant corralling. JB: That's a whole outlook, looking for the similarity instead of looking for the difference. There's a basic psychology theory that when you're outside a group, you notice how everybody in that group looks similar, but when you're within a group, you notice how everybody in your group is unique—how they differ from the others and yourself. It's a difference of perspective. From where you're standing, do you look more often for the differences or for the similarities? TO: Perspective leads us to our own versions of everything, I guess. But that theory makes sense, because from within, similarities are givens. It's your differences that are the fun parts, the parts that add the spark to it. Who wants

to be with yourself all the time? But you have to find a balance. As much as I make these things to amuse myself, I'm well aware of the link that must be created between the consumer and what I do. So I have to present the platform so that it's accessible, by making it either in a shape or in some sort of color or texture or something that someone somehow has a link to, and then I can present a new idea, a new concept, a new fit. But all the way odd, or all around where people can't relate to it, that makes it very hard to understand and therefore it makes it impractical, and I hate things when they're not practical. When you're making something like clothes, it has to be accessible to some person. JB: Incorporating something familiar in order to showcase something new sounds almost like visual analogy. You have to use an analogy for somebody to relate to something, and all of a sudden they say, "Oh, I get it." TO: Basically it's just an abuse of already established systems, and trying to see it as a fresh approach. All of my design is based on conservative starts, and then where it ends up obviously isn't in the same terrain. I really love preppy, conservative clothes, and it's fun to be able to tweak them. I think they're the most finely tuned, proven way to dress. There's usually a reason something's been around forever: It really works. So you take the

Above: Hand-embroidered top with glass beads and raffia in Indian-flourished patchwork inspired by Li'l Abner's Daisy May, spring 1992. Opposite: Bird Top, opalescent sequins and beads on linen for a wrinkled effect, spring 1992.

practicality, and then the thrill of departure—and it's always fun to make uptight people nervous, anyway. For example, to make a fabric for the spring 1993 collection, we went to a tie manufacturer in England. This mill was three hundred years old; they do the rep ties, the classic British striped ties, for all the English school systems. You can't get more conservative than that! When manufacturers show you what they can do, they have what they call a blanket, which is a woven patchwork of all the different patterns they make. You look at the blanket and you choose among the patterns. Well, I wanted the blanket itself—all the patterns at once. And they were delighted to work with us. It opened up all sorts of new ideas for them. Three hundred years of the same thing—can you imagine? And then somebody comes in and wants you to do all this freaky stuff. They were very happy about it. JB: That's a great example of not starting from scratch, of coming in the middle but still having stuff to do. TO: I love that. When you get to these old systems, and somebody says, "Oh no, it works this way, we only do it this way," and you get in there and just change their system a little bit, and then you get something they've never seen before, something totally fresh by just being willing to work somewhat within their boundaries to get something new. With machinery, it's like getting to take the radio apart and put it back together. As a kid, I was constantly disassembling—or dismembering, however you want to look at it—anything electronic. What's in there? At our factory, we've sanded down cams, and pulled off things, and ground up things to get whole other stitches that you wouldn't necessarily get. Or to duplicate certain looks that were done by hand, so you can do it by machine because you screwed with it. JB: It's funny that we now work at injecting that handmade touch by making a machine do what it's not supposed to do, so that it's not as consistent. After working so hard to create machines, now we want things to look like they're done by hand after all. TO: That's often my first advice to clients when I consult for these huge firms, is please try to make it look like a human hand touched it, because I think there's a real sadness involved with automation today. People don't necessarily want it to be all by machine. I like to think that humans had something to do with it. I also see it as a new cultural phenomenon. There's a desire to downscale the world, or at least to feel like it's downscaled. Everything got too electronic, too corporate, too machine-made. It'll be interesting to see how far it'll go. It's the removal, the stripping away. It's gotten too automated. We are people. We have different desires than machinery alone can supply.

It's

your

differences

that are

the

fun parts

the

parts

that

add

the

spark

to

it

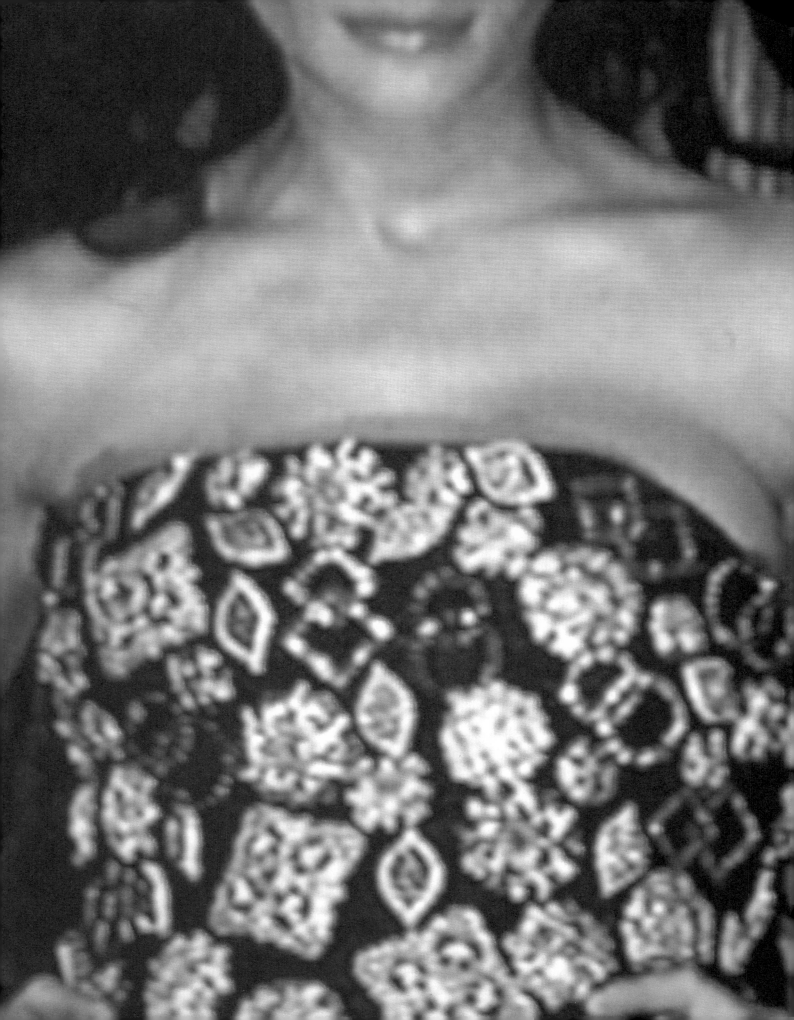

i

have

a

boundary

a very

loose

boundary

called

"clothes"

how

do

i

approach

it

?

happy mistakes

I met Todd just before his first collection, which showed at Pratt about eleven years ago. I remember listening to Prince's album *Around the World in a Day* for the first time with him. I remember that first collection well. At the time I thought it was very "disco glam," and what I saw still has relevance today. Since then his output has been voluminous and has helped to resurrect print design and the daringness to use color, especially in contrast to the thoughtful minimalism of the Japanese and American designers. His prints and beadwork have become a signature characteristic of his collections, similar in sensibility and opulence to Christian Lacroix. His experimentation does not stop at decorative considerations, but also explores proportion in the relationship between garment and body. His cuts are engineered in a unique way that redefines the figure. The negative space in a dress may become a window to the body or a texture in a striped pattern. Todd seems to approach fashion from a nonfashion point of view. He draws from the whole of culture, especially in terms of print and imagery. He finds beauty in the most unexpected places and is able to draw from a very large pool of information. We live in a landscape of complete opportunity—everywhere you turn, you could perceive something as "art," depending on how you crop a view or see one thing juxtaposed with another. Billboards next to buildings next to signs next to trees—the weird, eclectic mix of imagery that's especially prevalent in urban centers. Todd reinterprets and applies those kinds of elements in much of what he does. Everything can be used in some way, and Todd's a great example of someone utilizing information that others might discard. It's not necessarily the thing itself that's valuable, but the relationship the observer has to the thing. Todd doesn't just reproduce an outside element; he reconceives its setting, which is what distinguishes his work from kitsch. He might be appropriating something from the so-called low, but he elevates it with the context he provides, redefining elements from his environment and integrating them into his personal vision. I have come to think of Todd more as a "pop conceptual engineer" than a clothing designer. When I collaborate with Todd, his imagery provides me with material to redefine in the graphic medium. It's like playing with flashcards or editing a movie—the juxtapositions yield their own impact, changing our perspective toward one element based on what precedes or follows it. When working with material from diverse sources, the relationship between the elements is what transforms the original. It is the remix that interests me. Todd and I both work from an intuitive level; we're trying to release the information that appears on our interior screens. Without much talk, we are able to tap into similar information and work within a context that also allows for the happy mistake. My desire is to highlight Todd's work, and to magnify the parts that resonate between us. —Tom Bonauro

Page 83: Arizona Highway Print, featuring pictures from *Arizona Highway* magazine, spring 1994. Above: Untitled, oil on silver leaf, detail, 1990. Opposite: Nikki Umberti wearing gold stretch-lamé Baked Potato Dress, spring 1994. Photograph by Steen Sundland.

JB: Is there a common denominator to what you like about other people's art? TO: Presence and reverence. I think those two things are absolutely most of what I appreciate in art, and what I see around me in the art I've collected. Diane Arbus has been such a leading inspiration to me for years because she didn't come from the worlds she depicted, yet she had great reverence for them and offered a version of that to many people through her work without being exploitative. And I think, in bridging worlds like that, it's an exact metaphor for what I do. JB: What are the worlds that you're bridging? TO: Well, I bridge all kinds of worlds that aren't normally seen in fashion. Fashion design—which is a vague term—is mainly considered to be highbrow, with highbrow references, made for people who are highbrow, who have money to afford it. So fashion designers go for tasteful things, since there's the notion that high fashion is an upper-echelon entity. Because I also love trailer parks, and maybe a nasty old acrylic blanket, but then also adore Moorish architecture, I incorporate a broader focus into my work. So it's really a mishmash of these disparate worlds that wouldn't necessarily be across the street from each other. But in my life, they are. JB: You seem especially to appreciate art that comes from beyond the mainstream, outsider art. TO: What I think of as outsider art isn't its general definition. Outsider art usually means more naive art, like matchstick or hobo art. I respond to artwork from the impassioned eye that is not necessarily coming from the main systems. Technically, art-historically speaking, Arbus did not do outsider art, but the way I see it, I think it is. JB: In what ways does Arbus's work affect your own vision? TO: Her passion toward her subjects reminds me to incorporate constant thrill and inspiration. The imagery itself is sublime, but the integrity and power and passion behind it is the inspiration. JB: You've also talked about the modernist furniture and objects of Ray and Charles Eames as influences. It seems like there would be a big difference between an Arbus inspiration and an Eames inspiration. TO: But they're not very different for me. Clearly the end results look very different, but they were both produced with the same ingenuity and love for their subject and their medium, and they're all masterful at what they do. Arbus almost seems to shoot in between the moment. She seems to catch that sliver of a moment before or after the real picture. And with the Eameses, I really appreciate the practical points of view. You know, they started molding wood when they were designing splints during World War II— a totally functional endeavor, but they actually made those beautiful as well. Everything they did was based on total practicality to be some of the most

Above: Red vinyl Scooter Santa Suit, fall 1993. Photograph by Matthew Rolston. Opposite: Todd Oldham Jeans, laminated denim, spring 1995. Photograph by Gilles Bensimon.

deliciously silly, impractical-looking things, like those funny chairs that were kind of lopsided. They don't look practical at all, and yet they're engineered so perfectly that they work great. I relate from the heart to what the Eameses did, because everything was functional, yet they put lightness and whimsy and joy and love and practicality into everything they did, and they were so multifaceted. They had an umbrella that any product or sensibility or concept could fly out from under. I hope to set my life up to be a studio in the way that they did. JB: I would think that the translation process of the inspiration would differ, though. The Eameses' work seems to be more readily applicable in terms of tangible properties, the appreciation for the hand-crafted and the function. Arbus's work, of course, is not functional. TO: Yeah, the inspirations can be applied in different ways. But it's the passion that's the fuel, really. You may learn a technical trick or two from the Eameses—but I can't even say that, because I look in the same way at the light streaks in some of Arbus's photos. Clearly she didn't intend them to be there, but they create some of the magic. There's one picture of a woman holding a cross with a light streak right across the middle. It was obviously a camera mistake, but it's really otherworldly and meant to be. And the proper framing eye is so essential. JB: Is there any art in which you can't find the beauty?

TO: Art for art's sake, where it's totally passionless—like, I need that painting for my sofa, therefore it has to have blue in it. That, for me, is art for art's sake. It's not a matter of talent. Maybe that makes me a little bit haughty, to require that what's behind the art be of the same integrity as the piece itself. But it's just so important to me, I can't overlook that. JB: That loss of passion is often what happens when you do something over and over again without changing it. TO: It's pure commerce at that point. There's really no other artistic bent to it. That's why I find myself in awe of people who express themselves simply for the means of expression—and of the times when I'm able to do that. You can always see when something's been fueled by passion, whether you appreciate the style or not. You can tell what went into it. And it's the singularity—that's why paint-by-numbers is such a cool medium. Because even though the format's set up, no matter what—no matter what—you have the only one. I like that. Due to your lack of skill, or your anal-retentive tendencies, or whatever, that painting is yours and yours alone. JB: Within those boundaries I bet you can see the individual touch more clearly, because you know what somebody was working with, and you can see differences within those known, common parameters. It would be really interesting to give a bunch of people the same paint-by-numbers kits

Page 88: Todd Oldham Jeans, fall 1996. Photograph by Gus Van Sant. Page 89: Paint-by-Numbers Horse Print, detail, spring 1991.

87

and look at the finished paintings all together. TO: Actually, I've done an informal study like that just by collecting the same ones over and over. I have four or five of the same ones and they're all totally different. You can also see mistakes from the manufacturer, when they transposed the numbers on the paintboxes—there's this whole series with lime green and purple deer, and I have couple of those. JB: What I like about things like paint-by-numbers, or those paper-doll boxes you found, is that it seems like everybody must have their outlet, their weird way of expressing themselves. Sometimes it's something familiar in which they invest passion, like gardening or cooking, but other times there are these really bizarre, fetishistic outlets that almost feel like guerrilla creativity. TO: It's exactly that compulsion that I love. Because now I create for the most part with some attachment to commerce, and even though I'm still able to be fulfilled in much the same way as if I was creating outside of commerce, for me I could just sit and have all those ideas in my head. They wouldn't have to come out. Just to think it is as much as painting it or making it or seeing it in some tangible form, which isn't important to me. So I really appreciate people who never wavered from their intense love of a particular subject matter. JB: You talk about fine art, scavenged, theoretical, or life influences a lot, but don't you have any specific inspirations that come from fashion?

TO: Well, it would have to be catalogs—Sears, Penney's, Montgomery Ward. I don't remember seeing fashion magazines until I was about twelve or thirteen, or being aware of them before. And they just seemed weird—they didn't make sense in the way that Sears made sense. Sears catalogs are really cool, especially the old ones. We looked at Sears catalogs as just Christmas wishbook kind of stuff, but they were, through the eyes of the Sears company, the most perfectly homogenized and filtered things they could come up with, because their goal was to meet everyone's needs. So what you got was basically a boiled-down view of design history at the moment the catalog was printed. As social studies, they're quite fascinating. JB: But how do you reconcile the homogeneity of the Sears catalog with your appreciation for integrity and individuality? TO: Well, at the time Sears was the only thing I knew. That was the originality. But I could tell, after looking at something for a while, that those were not the original ideas. So in a way it motivated me to find out where the real ideas came from, to seek the truth and integrity. In one of the catalogs the company pictured the original next to their reproduction—there were loads of Eames knockoffs, actually—and they'd say, "Ours is only $17.99!" But the real one was always better somehow. So maybe they weren't so much the inspiration because of integrity, but more inspiration for integrity.

Above: Beaded button, holiday 1994. Opposite: Susan Sarandon wearing hand-tie-dyed, crushed-velvet suit, fall 1994. Photograph by Guzman. Pages 92–93: Amber Valetta wearing gold duchesse-satin tight blouse, and Nadja Auermann wearing white duchesse-satin jacket with powder blue Swarovski crystal bra, spring 1994—the form of the bra is based on censor bars.

Opposite: Uma Thurman wearing jeweled Tuft Print gown, fall 1992. Photograph by Sheila Metzner. Page 96: Untitled, oil and thread on paper, detail, 1988. Page 97: Chandra North wearing Todd Oldham Jeans, denim with Tuft Print interior, spring 1992. Photograph by Joshua Jordan.

the
m—
x

Todd Oldham, in both personality and design, represents pure Americana. When Todd first made a blip on the international fashion radar he was sort of a UFO. His persona is a hybrid of Pee Wee Herman and Howdy Doody, steeped in a broth of Schiaparelli. In short, he's the antithesis of the impossibly regal European couturiers and self-aggrandizing Seventh Avenue moguls whose bloated public profiles are sometimes better constructed than their designs. When I think about Todd, it's not his wealth, Hollywood friends, personal scandals, or ridiculous fashion dictums like "stars are the new stripes" that come to mind—it's his clothes. Todd's designs are both exhilaratingly original and eerily derivative in the same way as hip-hop music. Influences drawn from junior high arts-and-crafts projects, such as decoupage; jailhouse art with its labor-intensive accessories; or such lowbrow pleasures as spin art—all find their way into his postmodern palette. There's no tiresome, arcane nostalgia in his work that would force both model and consumer to aspire to a world in which they have never or can never live. His garments are not standard price-tag uniforms meant to validate the woman by the obvious display of a logo. I love Todd's work for its accurate immediacy. I'm always amazed at his affinity for and celebration of wild-style urban expression and proportion. The abandon of club culture figures strongly in his collections. He makes garments that recall the movements of jungle music, raves, and acid house, nights at the Paradise Garage and the Roxy, where the good times do nothing but roll. Todd has no fear of flourish, so at one turn you might be given the secret ego boost of panties that look like a Puerto Rican wedding cake, or you might get a filthy-cute pair of pedal pushers that make you feel like Rizzo, the bad girl with a heart of gold in *Grease*. Walking his runways I gave some of my more inspired performances as a model. I attribute this not so much to the party atmosphere of his shows, but instead to his design formula. As a model, I've often felt as though I was enfolded in some delicate piece of origami that could betray me at any moment, or I was completely overwhelmed by what the designer's logo was meant to represent. Both situations could make my body personality shrink exponentially with every little step I took. But wearing Todd's clothes gave me an unwavering confidence to express any aspect of my personality, because I didn't feel overwhelmed by the cut of the clothes. Even though Todd bases every collection on the functional premises of sportswear or preppy dressing, he's a high-concept designer. The fabrics, prints, and themes have a uniqueness alien to conventionality, but the feel and the look of the clothes are not alienating to the person wearing them. Having worn Todd's clothes on the runway and in real life, I can testify that he invents looks for women who live. And I mean women who live fiercely. I've made speeches about breast cancer and AIDS wearing Todd Oldham outfits. Executed grand entrances at snooty society soirees. Hiked one of his dresses up so I could disco down, balled it up and thrown it in the corner, and then fallen out of bed a triumphant seductress to slip the dress on again, slinking out onto the street in the wee hours of dawn, fabulous as ever. Todd is one of the great democrats of fashion. Gay, straight, fat, thin, grunge, hip hop—no matter what kind of consumer you are (and believe me, I've seen it all in action), wearing a Todd Oldham is like holding a winning lottery ticket.

—Veronica Webb

Page 98: Flame Print, spring 1994. Page 99: Repainting, 1992—I added the birds to this old found portrait. Above: Found scrapbook detail, 1950s. Opposite: Michelle Hicks wearing vinyl and fake fur Snowbunny Costume, fall 1993. Photograph by Raymond Meier.

JB: Did your creative expression start with clothes? TO: Not really. I just see this clothing thing as a part of it. It's not the whole of my expression. It's been the most profitable of all the things I've done, but it's no different for me from when I made terrariums in the seventh grade, or when I embroidered on crepe paper with yarn. It's all the same. One just has a little more commerce attached to it, or has tangible commercial outlets. JB: How did you originally get the idea to do clothes as your first effort that would be commercial? TO: Clothing seemed not to be the easiest necessarily, but it offered the most immediate results out of all the stuff I did. Even in the fourth grade when I was making purses out of hair ribbons and felt, it was easy to sell them and it was accessible to others, so when I wanted to make something that would allow me to eat, clothes sort of worked out. It was never the thing that I lived to do. It still isn't. Maybe that's where I get my perspective. JB: Besides the commercial aspects of designing clothes, is there anything else that differentiates it from other creative outlets? TO: You're designing something that— and I guess this could be up for debate—should be functional. That's the cool part. You're creating within an arena that does have a few boundaries. A lot of people like to be able to stand and sit when they have clothes on! JB: So function is a boundary that you like.

TO: Not that I like, but that I accept. But really, function is more a matter of format than boundary. JB: As opposed to preconceived notions about the way things should be? TO: Exactly. "Our customers want this." Yeah, well, they do want this now, but you're making clothes for a year and a half from now. So give them a little bit of what they want and then anticipate their needs. JB: And do what you like to design. TO: That's the thing, because anything goes these days. If you make it lovely, it's valid. That's all that matters now. JB: One of the striking things to me about your clothing is that many people wouldn't necessarily wear it, either due to financial constraints or because it's not their style, but they still seem to appreciate what you do from afar. To me, it's the pleasure of getting to see a really interesting thought process at work. TO: I'm certainly very happy that people respond well to my work, and I'm thrilled that people can appreciate it without having to buy it, without having to desire it. Because with something as subjective as clothing, it's pretty much either yes or no as to whether you want to wear it. So I'm happy to be a part of "That's so lovely, I don't want it." Because it means you've crossed over and invited another group of thinkers in. That's the best thing about what I do, is that someone could feel happy or aroused by it. Even if you don't like it, you can at least

Page 102: Jamie Wall wearing Horse Shirt, Todd Oldham Jeans, fall 1996. Photograph by Gus Van Sant. Page 103: Untitled, thread and oil, 1992. Opposite: Collage for *SoHo Journal,* made from Sears catalog cutouts and Chinese stationery, 1985. Above: Embroidered blouse, flower detail, spring 1993.

appreciate that there's some new thought involved. At least we're not boring you. JB: Do you have a personal favorite collection that you ever did? TO: Definitely. Spring 1993. It's the one I worked absolutely the most on. It was a big shift for me. There was a surrender during that season, because it was the most personalized effort I ever made. I put everything into that collection, in a way I hadn't before. Everything was custom-made—all the textiles, special linings that maybe you wouldn't see. We even made all the buttons, out of Creepy Crawler sets from when I was a kid. Creepy Crawlers are this highly dangerous child's toy that I'm sure has absolutely been pulled off the market. I'm surprised any of us had fingertips left after playing with this hideous toy. It consisted of a heated metal box, and a little metal tray that had deembossed images of things like bugs or flowers. You poured this highly toxic goop in the tray, and cooked it in the box until you had these soft rubbery toys. So we took advantage of these really cool metal molds. I think of spring 1993 as the crescendo of my bothering to bother, which is something I first noticed as a kid in Iran, somebody bothering to bother. To think that a man would devote basically his life's work to just the facade of the entrance of one building with the most intricate inlay— it was so great that someone bothered to bother. Because very few people bother to bother—it takes a lot of time and effort. I think that was really instrumental at the beginning of my career: People could tell

I bothered to bother. JB: What were some of the special things that you bothered to do? TO: Oh, I really went to town on this collection. There was an embroidery based on ancient Indian motifs and another on Fragonard paintings, beadings taken from Moroccan tile patterns, prints based on Egyptian tomb paintings. We spent so much time printing a harlequin fabric that we used just for linings. With one dress, we had sequins made into flower shapes, then we applied them in a flower pattern. So the sequin itself was shaped like a little daisy, and then to mimic the pattern of flowers in a shape that's flowers—I loved how . . . "solipsistic" is the wrong word, because that means it goes into itself, but it's almost like some version of pixelation. At first, looking at a television, you see an image, but when you get up on top of it, you see that it's composed of dots. But here the dots were the thing itself as well as the sum of the dots. And then mixing luscious textures and prints—there was one knit that I had duplicated from this hideous acrylic afghan I found in a drugstore near Las Vegas, but it had the most beautiful, classic shell stitch. There was another top where we knit together two different yarns, lime green and moss green, so you got this strange iridescent quality. I love tonal things, and knitting the two yarns as one creates a visual trick where the shadow become darker, which is a great way to punctuate body curves. And there were so many engineering marvels. Spring 1993 had the most complicated print we ever did, one blouse for

Above: Box for Todd Oldham Watches by Fossil, cedar and flocked animal, fall 1995. Opposite: Outtake from campaign for Todd Oldham Perfume, detail, 1993.

which every size required a separate printing because it was flawlessly engineered around every single section. Every dart, every border, the elbow patches—since all the details were printed, they had to be in a slightly different place for every size. It was very, very tricky, and the factory wanted to shoot me afterward. But we did it, and I've never seen anyone else do it, which is rare in this industry. JB: What did people notice in the show? Are you ever surprised by what people focus on? TO: Actually, it was interesting—there were two outfits that got highly noted, two solid dresses. There was no pattern, no shocking color, but people were happy to see a really sophisticated silhouette from us that wasn't involving a lot of activity. JB: They must also have stood out for their simplicity.

TO: Yeah, I suspect you could say of most other designers' shows that it would be the loud thing that would pop out. You know, even though spring 1993 was very special, I think it was overdose, because you can overwhelm people. At the time we did this, there wasn't a lot of the talent that's around now. People just didn't do things like we did then, so it was a really jarring collection that in many ways did not compute for some people. But the folks who came back to the showroom to have a look-see were excited by all we'd put into it. Because it was just more than you could ever think of. JB: You must have a real following among people who know what these things are, who know what kind of engineering and craft goes into the construction, the detail, and things like beading and printing. TO: We definitely get that—which is a great irony considering that probably most of the people who really appreciate what we do have no interest in wearing these sorts of things. Tiny little engineering means so much to me, but I wonder sometimes whether the people who do buy the clothes notice or appreciate a detail, or whether they have no idea it's even there. JB: I would think it would be the kind of thing you'd see over time. The way it feels, and little revelations you notice after you've had something for a while. You knew you loved it when you bought it, but then noticing the details is like finding explanations for things after you've already done them. You've already bought it because you liked it. It's like time-release gratification. TO: How nice that we have that autopilot response system. If you could just finely tune it, you wouldn't have to think at all. You could just do and do. That would be nice, but then maybe that would be boring, too. JB: It'd be nice to have a little of both. Because otherwise we'd have nothing to talk about. TO: Thoughts are our friends! JB: Pro-thoughts—the new campaign and bumper sticker. You could forge a coalition between the pro-thoughts and the pro-feelings forces and you'd have it all covered. TO: And pro-choice. JB: The pros! All the pros. TO: Except the pro-athletes. That's another story.

Above: Lifesaver Gown, beads and sequins, detail, fall 1994. Opposite: UFO photos, black-and-white Polaroids taken for *SoHo Journal*, 1994.

Top and bottom: Untitled, oil on thread and leaf, details, 1992. Opposite: Nadja Auermann wearing Mosaic Print day dress, spring 1994. Photograph by Steven Klein. Page 112: Stacey McKenzie wearing Todd Oldham Jeans, fall 1996. Photograph by Gus Van Sant. Page 113: Untitled, oil and silver leaf on Persian newspaper, 1990.

high

and

low

One Sunday morning many years ago, I was wandering through the Twenty-sixth Street flea market obsessing over whether I should buy these three ridiculously bad art-school oil paintings of the American presidents Washington, Lincoln, and Kennedy. I had seen them minutes before for ten dollars each, and I remember thinking it was a fine line—they were so hideous that they were either fabulous or horrible, and I couldn't decide which. Thank God fifteen minutes later I ran into Todd, who was on the ground rummaging through a cardboard box filled with old curtains. After saying our hellos-we're-working-so-hard-we-never-see-each-other, I asked him to come with me to see if I was insane to buy these three big, really hideola and imposing portraits. He looked at the paintings and, in a split second, looked back at me and said, "If you don't buy them, Kim, I will." Well, I got out my thirty dollars so fast the seller didn't know what hit him. I learned my lesson in taste, and the paintings have of course become three of my favorites. Todd's clothes, which are sexy, pro-women, and funny, have always gone much deeper than what meets the eye. Todd has always incorporated inspirations from his many obsessions and his true Texas grass roots into his collections. Those curtains in that cardboard box at the flea market probably ended up as a print for one of his dresses, as most likely did a shower curtain he found on Fourteenth Street or his favorite paint-by-numbers still life. When he tie-dyed velvet for gowns, it was done upstate by hippie folks and not imitated in some Seventh Avenue workroom. Fabrics for shirts and jackets might be

photoprints of clutter swiped from his employees' desks. Or they could be taken from paintings by some of his talented friends. Todd's brother makes the funky buttons for his shirts and his mom runs the factory. Although these nuances are usually missed by a fashion industry that sees his work as clothing on the rack, Todd doesn't really care much. He has always found himself just on the outside—and maybe even on his way out of this fashion world anyway. For Todd, fashion is definitely just the tip of the iceberg. Prolifically making his art in as many mediums as possible is what's really important to him. His vision—whether sewn in clothes, painted on canvas, politicized, filmed, or even handicrafted and decorated—is consistent. It is ironic that fashion has brought Todd Oldham fame—so much so that he can barely even show his Opie-face-made-famous-by-MTV at the flea market anymore—because it is regular folk, not movie stars, to whom he has always gravitated for inspiration. But then again, Todd Oldham himself is an outsider, which is what I love about him and which is what makes him stand apart from the others. Whether making fashion away from Seventh Avenue and its expectations and rules, coming from outside the art scene to show artwork in a gallery, or bypassing the film industry and venturing into filmmaking sideways, his sonar for steering away from the hype types in any kind of business has always been bull's-eye. Although we're not sure what direction Todd will decide to go in next, we do know that it will surely be bullshit-free, radical in its thought, and outside the mainstream. Thank God. —Kim Hastreiter

Page 114: Airbrushed Disk Print, fall 1996. Page 115: Every spring 1994 print worn all at the same time. Photograph by Gilles Bensimon. Above: Collage for German *Max*, detail, 1994. Opposite: Jennifer Jason Leigh wearing study of layered transparencies with striped stretch-silk panties, spring 1996. Photograph by Kate Garner, 1996. Photographed for *Entertainment Weekly*. Pages 118–119: Kristin McMenamy leading parade of Chinese floral ensembles, spring 1995.

JB: Does it inspire you creatively to work in different media, moving from painting to clothes to interior spaces and architecture to film? TO: I've come to totally love it. I realize it's the reason I'm able to do so many things, if only because it's a way to concentrate my short attention span. If I do four or five things in one day, I can do everything really easily. If I had to do one thing all day long, it would be really laborious. JB: Moving from medium to medium must keep you supple, staving off atrophy. TO: Oh, yeah. You stay limber. But it's a way of life you learn. I think of it like the gymnastics I did as a kid—I have no reason to be as limber as I am now, but because I was trained as a kid, my body's remembered. So through the way I operate with creativity, I'm trained to stay open. JB: Do you learn from one medium and then apply to another? TO: Absolutely. Everything I'm thinking about has been changed right now because I've been designing a hotel in Miami. I'm responding to many more things from a modernist viewpoint than I ever would have before, and it's just because I've been studying architecture. JB: What's the modernist point of view to you? TO: Well, for me it's not so much the modernists' total point of view, but their clean aesthetic sensibilities that I've really been enjoying—finding out how much a little can mean. People still see masters practicing this, but now it's being done with whimsy. Usually you don't see stark elements like modern design combined with whimsy. Charles and Ray Eames were masters of humane modernism. JB: Humane meaning not-so-dictatorial modernism, as opposed to a Mies van der Rohe building? TO: Well, even that's kind of lovely, but I've never seen a Mies van der Rohe sofa that you wanted to go plop down on. JB: It was also so dictatorial, like, You have to have the same color Levolors as everybody else otherwise you're evicted. TO: Exactly. It's a funny point of view. But that exists in the fashion industry, too. There are always fascists in every arena. But I'm realizing that simple things are often the hardest to do, because the fine-tuning must be so masterful. It's a trick. I do appreciate aspects of minimalism, but I don't know that it's our natural instinct as humans. It seems to be forced. Luis Barragan is a huge influence, especially with color—the sheer braveness of doing a five-foot hot pink wall with color so true it looks like pure pigment. And then juxtaposing it with rust. Rust and hot pink—what's more beautiful? And why not five stories of it? JB: Is there a way to put ornate, baroque sensibilities into modernism? That seems to me something you could really bring to it, like Barragan introducing color. TO: Definitely. What I like about any movement is to see how it crosses other boundaries, because there seems to be a synergy between all styles, when you really get in there and look. So it's fun to see what the common

Above: Dan Rienzi wearing Todd Oldham Jeans, fall 1996. Opposite: Sexy outdoor outfit of stretch vinyl and polar fleece, Todd Oldham Jeans, fall 1996. Photographs by Gus Van Sant.

denominators are, and how they cross almost every genre. Especially in architecture and furniture design. You can see how, for example, the backbone structures of some of the Eames chairs could mimic some tiny part of a molding or cross at Versailles. **JB: You're moving into filmmaking now. What draws you in that direction?** TO: It was actually the only thing I knew I wanted to do from the very beginning. I'm still debating whether to be involved in clothes or not, but I always knew I wanted to work with movies. When I was a kid living in Iran, I cut out every *New York Times*, *Time,* and *Newsweek* review and stuck it in a notebook. **JB: Was it the fantasy that fascinated you originally? TO:** No, it was always the technical stuff, which I could see right off the bat. I could understand cuts, why people would edit there to punch up an emotion. I instinctively stripped it back, so I was rarely able to fall for it. For some reason when I saw what was on the screen, I could always picture what was ten feet around it, what the screen wasn't revealing. I could see the periphery of activity. I got so involved in the technical aspects I didn't get as wrapped up in the story, and it's still that way. Though when I saw *Lolita* for the first time, in junior high, it really stunned me. It came on TV, so I'm sure it was cut to bits, but it really moved me because I realized the importance of storytelling. Because *Lolita* is a little

story; nothing really sweeping happens, so it's all in the telling. That movie is just so weird, so wicked and funny at the same time, which stirred up a lot of emotions in me as a kid. **JB: Do you tell stories in your clothes? TO: Sure.** Even if no one knows what the story is, the process is the storytelling. You put a little of this in, a little of that—it's like a recipe. **JB: Moving from medium to medium reminds me of translating imagery. It's sort of what I enjoy about speaking other languages—by necessity, finding other ways to express things. You often represent the same things in different generations, like taking a painting and reproducing it in a sequined skirt, and then color-xeroxing it, and then maybe taking a photograph of the color xerox, with new things in every representation.** TO: Oh, definitely. You couldn't do it in a more roundabout way, but what an adventure. The best for me was like you said, with that one print where we color-xeroxed the beading. It was really exciting to start seeing the gleams and the way that was removed—it just seemed so multilevel because beading's all about texture, you know? And sequins are about texture and shine, so we eliminated every bit of that existence. **JB: Rather than trying to faithfully reproduce everything, you move from one generation to another, from one reproduction to another, making everything, no matter what you do, be its own thing.**

Opposite: Naomi Campbell and Nadja Auermann wearing sterling silver and Swarovski crystal Stripper Bras, spring 1994. Above: Opening shot for "Todd Time" segment on MTV's *House of Style*, designed by Tom Bonauro.

TO: Oh, definitely. You have to make sure everything lives up to its own-thingness. I don't mind subtle variations, as long as it's not variation in function—I don't want it to be broken. It's always nice when something feels like it's the only one, the same satisfaction from singularity in art as from moments in time and personal experience. JB: It seems like you're moving toward more theoretical inspirations. As I look over the course of your work, there are very tangible stylistic ideas, like something from Morocco, a tile pattern maybe, but now when you discuss what enthuses you, it's much more about concepts, such as modernism. TO: I think that's definitely true. Inspiration is like a door—the more you open it, the more there's another door behind it that leads you to the next door, all the time. For

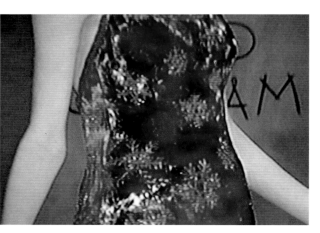

some reason I've been opening the doors faster these days, growing and being really excited by and open to things that had never tickled my eye before. I think it's from architecture. JB: Which you didn't process as much before? TO: I always looked at architecture for inspiration, but I was never responsible for concrete elements such as electrical schematics. Now that I'm designing interior spaces, I've been examining architecture with a really serious eye. JB: What do you think about when you're designing a space? TO: It's the same as clothing: Start with practical notions, and then apply the rest. If I'm designing a physical space, whether my home or my stores or something for somebody else, I love to immediately dig in with what's practical. People have to sit here, they have to get by—there are just a million things to think of. So once all the practical stuff gets in, then I move to all the fun stuff. To create a space that's service-oriented is really exciting. But that doesn't mean it's not spontaneous. The store we just opened in Miami was absolutely the most spontaneous store we ever did, and in the end came out to be the very most lovely and fine-tuned and best-made store we ever did. JB: It surprises me to hear you say spontaneous, because it seems so well thought out and polished. TO: It's the liquid organic flow of design that comes from working with a great team. Obviously there are plans. Somebody has to think about all the structure stuff, but then you just trust that things will turn out well because you're working with great people. In Miami, unlike with the other stores where we bought a few things premade, we made every single thing. And I mean everything—from the doorknobs to the chandeliers. It's just evolved that way. Before we would try to buy a few things, but I was never as happy with something I bought as with one I made, so we continue to go with that. I figured it out—at this point, I thankfully know of enough great people that we really can get

Above: Beaded Snowflake Gown, detail, fall 1994. Opposite: Chandra North and Mark Cunningham wearing Todd Oldham Jeans, lying on thousands of hand-painted leaves, spring 1995. Photograph by Joshua Jordan.

anything made. JB: You've chosen some of the most collaborative mediums to express yourself in—filmmaking, clothes, architecture or interior design—as opposed to more solitary pursuits, such as painting or sculpture. TO: There's nothing more fun than working with a lot of people who are good. And that makes all the difference, working with good people versus unskilled ones. But the ability to collaborate also depends on what you're expecting from the outcome of your vision. Sometimes the lack of control within the group effort, handing things over to other people's hands, is really exciting. I'm just as happy to be a part of something as I am to be the sole originator, if I'm doing it with the right people. JB: What do you want a space you design to feel like? TO: I think when you approach any project, you have to be considerate to your invited guests and to your surroundings. The Miami store is probably a hundred yards from the ocean, so I felt a great obligation to be reverent to Mother Nature. I designed the whole floor to mimic the ocean. It looks like rolling waves. Why would I want to compete with something as beautiful as the ocean in Florida? You have to be considerate of where you are. It's like the way I approach jeans: You work within a proven format, a certain specific design genre, and then breathe your own version into it. Florida has such beautiful tile, and I'm a tile fiend, but

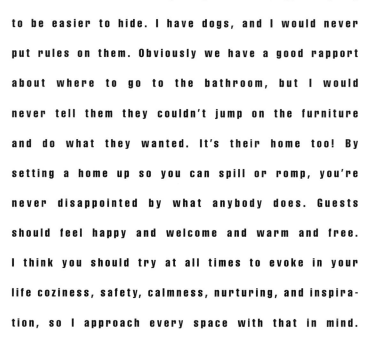

there's so much traditional tile down there that we wanted to do something different. We made our own tiles and sequenced and cut and mitered them on the spot for the store's fountains, and ended up with Moorish flourishes, but still feeling absolutely American, very "where you are." JB: What about a home? Would you approach a private space differently? TO: I think homes should be based on great comfort. Homes are very womblike; when it's so crazy outside, your home has to be very special. I like to capture the feeling that the parents aren't home. And when it's your own space, you have the opportunity to indulge a highly personalized sense of what you want to look at. But again, you want to think about being practical—like tie-dyeing slipcovers so if you spill something, it's going to be easier to hide. I have dogs, and I would never put rules on them. Obviously we have a good rapport about where to go to the bathroom, but I would never tell them they couldn't jump on the furniture and do what they wanted. It's their home too! By setting a home up so you can spill or romp, you're never disappointed by what anybody does. Guests should feel happy and welcome and warm and free. I think you should try at all times to evoke in your life coziness, safety, calmness, nurturing, and inspiration, so I approach every space with that in mind.

Opposite: Tyra Banks and Beverly Peele wearing the Interiors Collection, ensembles inspired by interior decoration, fall 1992. Photograph by Max Vadukul. Above: Tyra Banks wearing the Interiors Collection, fall 1992. Photograph by Gilles Bensimon.

Opposite, top: Karen Mulder wearing beaded Iceberg Dress with fake-polar-bear coat, fall 1994. Opposite, bottom: Anna wearing purple Toilet Seat-Cover Hat, fall 1993. This page: Keri Claussen wearing chenille robe with wrap top of gold thread and pearl macramé, fall 1994.

JB: You mentioned earlier that you were just as content to think something as to create it, that it didn't have to come out in tangible form. But what about the pleasure of actually creating? TO: I'm at the point now where I've seen enough physical manifestations of my ideas, and as much as I do love them, I know that I'm now content to just think them up. Because I know how to execute things, the process isn't as important to me now as it once was. So I don't see them in contrast—I see them as more simultaneous. At first, there was more of the joy of the creation, but now because I do so much of it, it's the ideas that really thrill me. It's commerce that allows me to manifest them. JB: What about the need and the desire to communicate your ideas? TO: I love the idea of communicating. It's obviously why we're here. But my personality makeup doesn't supply me with so much of a need to communicate verbally with people. I'm much happier to communicate through my efforts than through my spoken voice. What I most admire is the ability to create a singular moment, partly because the feeling of experiencing a singular moment is so great. To hear somebody sing a beautiful song that has entered your ear and now it's a part of your memory, and it doesn't exist in any other way. Maybe it's on vinyl somewhere, but the one you just heard coming out of their mouth is only for that moment. When I was about fourteen, we went to Thailand for Christmas, and it was my first trip to the

Far East. There were perfect, overwhelming moments where it was almost like being in an amphitheater of sensation. We went to see the Reclining Buddha, which is this enormous gold statue. Its feet were so amazing—the gold created this incredible gleam, and the soles had the most beautiful paintings that looked like circuitry from the transistor radios I used to take apart, or computer encoding, which made me wonder where these modern forms come from. The tourist book was telling us we were seeing this ancient relic, and to me it was looking like the future, almost from outer space. And there were huge offerings of big purple orchid sprays everywhere and enormous piles of burning incense. So to have orchid and incense smells and these wild thoughts, it was just happily dizzying. I think eyes can sometimes create limits. Smell is our strongest sense that can take us anywhere, no matter what life. There's also such immediacy with our ears. We hear things, maybe a voice but also the rustle of the bamboo and the sound of the wind, and all these add up to only this second in time. To me, it's about the celebration of our individual selves. All of our experiences are pretty much just our version of it, even if we're all in the same room. It's like those first times you realize that our experiences are singular. Even though we were all going to that school, and we all had to be home at three, and we all had to go to bed at nine, when I realized that I was the only person in the

Above: Emma S. and Anna wearing whirling dervish—inspired costumes, fall 1993. Opposite: Shalom Harlow wearing Positano tile print, spring 1995. Photograph by Arthur Elgort.

whole world standing on this piece of grass in this field right now it was such a relief to me. To see or hear something special now is like being able to experience those little singular pockets of time. JB: I can understand why you wouldn't be as interested in the making of an idea, but I think of you as so uniquely handy, so involved in the actual craft of what you do. Doesn't that manifest itself in your finished product? TO: It's one of the reasons my stuff doesn't look like other people's. JB: What's the line there between the creativity and the handiness? TO: I have no preconceived notions about procedure and the way things are done. Because I'm handy, I can get in there and experiment and try new ways. Otherwise I'd have to work with someone who would say, "This is how it's done." And I'd have to cooperate. I could make a good argument about why it shouldn't be done that way, but if I can do it myself, I sidestep all that bullshit. JB: Don't you enjoy actually fabricating things yourself? Rolling up your sleeves, working with the materials? TO: It's the best. I'm never happier than when I'm being a lumberjack and banging on stuff and gluing. I love it. JB: Do you have more of a feeling of accomplishment when you make something by yourself, as opposed to when you have somebody else do it for you? TO: For me, it's sometimes more fun to just design and see things executed later, but for the most part, at least for the first one, it's really fun to do it yourself. It's so satisfying to see

something come out of your hands. But it's more than that—because I'm open to a wild card here and there, I can usually get something I wasn't planning on. So I have to be there, working with the materials, to react and then move forward. It's really important to be present in the process. I love finding new techniques by accident. For example, in the Miami store, we hand-laid papers on the wall, some with gold flecks on them and some natural bark papers. But when we applied the polyurethane, it drew all of the pigment out of the paper and pulled the wood through it—and it looks like cork! So it's just this beautiful, magic texture there. JB: Are those on-the-spot surprises something you can make room for or let happen? TO: Totally. I think of them as happy mistakes. One of my favorites is when we spent much time engineering these dresses in a new stretch jersey that a manufacturer was doing exclusively for us. We'd made the patterns, which were very tricky, and when we got the fabric in, we sewed up the dresses. Two days later we came back, and we couldn't believe what we saw. The manufacturer hadn't finished the fabric properly, and it shrunk when it got into the heat, just from the air. These were supposed to be full-length dresses with complicated cutouts, one hole that started below the bust and moved down to show the navel, and a whole set of holes that went in the back. The holes shrunk up so much that they shifted to entirely different parts of the body, and the dresses were suddenly

Opposite: Tatjana Patitz wearing floor-length tiger ensemble, spring 1995. Photograph by Gilles Bensimon. Above: Screwy charm, silver plate with Swarovski crystal, spring 1992. Page 138, top: Amber Valetta, Kate Moss, and Shalom Harlow wearing Mosaic Print, spring 1994. Page 138, bottom: Tyra Banks wearing seed-beaded Xoaltchel gown, fall 1994. Page 139, top: Claudia Mason wearing diamond-ring bra with sequined tube top worn as skirt, spring 1994. Page 139, bottom: Keri Claussen wearing stretch satin bra and embroidered flower skirt, spring 1994.

knee-length. But we continued to work with them, and they came out quite nicely. JB: That must be very satisfying, to be able to turn a mistake into something exciting and new. Is there ever a dead end? Sometimes, however something works out is the way it should be. But I think of the creative process in some ways as being able to sustain you through trial and error when you hit the error. TO: I seek through trial; I never see the word "error" involved. A mistake might be costly, but I would never have gotten to the next step without it. Nothing feels like an error to me, because it was an explored concept. I learn through everything, so knowledge comes from any action to help with whatever the next action is. With that point of view, I never feel upset with myself about my ingenuity or my effort. Because I never set up any blocks to judge myself in a bad way, I can just proceed and it's real easy. Nothing new would ever come if people didn't make what other people think are mistakes. There's a Japanese concept called *wabi-sabi*—it's basically an antidote to modernism. It describes working with what others would deem as the major flaw, but instead of fretting about it, it's celebrating the flaw as the special element. If there was a crack in a beautiful piece of wood, you would work the wood and work the wood, concentrating on this one special crack and making it very beautiful. I think the

American version of this is a little bit more like a scavenger sensibility. Where the Japanese would use just one piece with a crack and the other pieces would be pristine in order to showcase the contradiction, we would use the flaw everywhere. So I sort of realized that everything I do is based on this wabi-sabi principle. I'm starting to understand what an important aspect of design this is! It's hard to articulate, but I think of wabi-sabi as an appreciation of a thing's special and inherent qualities without removing its singular characteristic, even though some might say that the singular characteristic is the flaw. JB: The way you describe wabi-sabi reminds me of the French term "jolie laide," which literally means "good-looking ugly woman." It's usually applied to women who aren't conventionally pretty but have a unique look and attractiveness and dignity, maybe from a striking imperfection. TO: What an important modern term. Because the beautiful and the ugly annul each other, to end up with something that just is. JB: If wabi-sabi is celebrating the one imperfection, it seems like you're always finding and celebrating the one pretty thing. TO: It's just finding the beauty. And seeing the beauty in all of it, really. JB: What visual optimism! TO: Oh, that's nice. I am a very optimistic person. You have to be. I mean, I have to be. I can't imagine existing without optimism.

Above: Debbie Dietering wearing beaded Crisscross Gown, detail, fall 1994. Opposite: Silk string and strapping sideview dress, spring 1994. Photograph by Raymond Meier. Page 142: Naomi Campbell wearing fake fur stole inspired by eccentric British dog trainer Barbara "No Bad Doggies!" Woodhouse, fall 1996. Page 143: Anna K. wearing sequined and beaded velvet T-shirt, fall 1996.

but began presenting his work to the public after high school.

Todd Oldham presented his first apparel collection in the fourth grade,

Tom Bonauro has a design studio in San Francisco and has collaborated with Todd,

both psychically and tangibly, on various projects. His work can be seen in the permanent collections of the

San Francisco Museum of Modern Art and the Smithsonian's Cooper-Hewitt Museum of Design in New York City.

Jen Bilik is a New York City writer and editor and, says Todd, an all-around great girl.

They are all still avoiding real jobs.